High Frequency Trading Systems

For the Covid Era

Using the Chauhan Actual Price in the E-Mini S&P 500
Futures

Vikram Singh Chauhan

High-Frequency Trading Systems For the Covid Era:
Using the Chauhan Actual Price in the E-Mini S&P 500
Futures

Vikram Singh Chauhan
Fort Worth, TX, USA

For information concerning any content of this work, please e-mail ChauhanCapitalManagement@gmail.com or follow my Twitter account @ChauhanCapital1.

Dedication

To my daughter Kensley

I will love you forever
and a day.
Yesterday, tomorrow, and
especially today.

Never forget that
if eternity ever
finds its end
my love for you
will still transcend.

Table Of Contents

Introduction

"Unprecedented" is a word that has become ubiquitous with the Covid era. Though it is an excessively used term it does an exceptional job of displaying the nature of how we quantify and qualify the financial markets and the economy, which is to say that they are relative. Phrases such as, "worst quarterly GDP drop on record", "highest unemployment rate since World War II", and "the Nasdaq broke its all-time high", display this. Their relative nature is expressed by anchoring to the beginning of a time frame, they are qualified by natural language objectives, and quantified by a "drop" or a "high".

Although I am a proponent of looking backward to look forward, I do not support regarding an "all-time" anything to inform me of a "right-now" something. This is not to say that data-tracking and record keeping are not of value, as such would be absurd. My point is, if we exist in an era of the unknown, how reliable is what we know? I postulate that it is not.

Instead I offer a shortened window of relativity in order to increase the efficiency in which we can call, ahead of time, the simplest of designations, Long or Short. In the ensuing pages I will offer a general overview of markets and concepts while offering mathematical formulas, binary entry signals, and computer code (EasyLanguage) for the reader to assess as they see fit.

I have great hope that we will emerge from the Covid Era stronger and better. This is how I regard the future of humanity, howbeit, I will regard my portfolio with an unreserved caution.

Acknowledgement

I would like to thank my mother Updesh for her unyielding support over these many painful years. Your love remains my guiding light. It has shown me the way through the darkness of the storm and the tumult of the open sea.

Thank you to my Little Sister Anita for help with formatting and being wonderful in dealing with my eccentricities and single-minded determination.

Also, the performance reports and signal testing would not have been possible without the help of my student and brother Roy Williams of East Sun Financial Group. We've come a long way and this is just the beginning.

Lastly, I would like to remember my Nani. You have left me with solid pronouncements of what I am, what I will be, and what you require of me. I will charge forward into this world while embodying your timeless and immortal words:

"I kick butt!"

What Is High-Frequency Trading?

High-frequency trading is a complex discipline that rests at the crossroads of the equally complex fields of high-frequency finance and computer science. Due to these complexities it is important to further specify the similarities and differences in key industry terms that tend to be associated, correctly or incorrectly, with HFT.

Systematic trading refers to computer driven trading decision that may be held for timeframes of between one month and one minute. Because there is a potential to allow a security holding period threshold to exceed its maximum of one day it could or could not be considered HFT. A systematic trading system would use a computer program to run daily, weekly, or even monthly data, would accept closing prices, and outputs portfolio allocation matrices that place buy-and-sell orders.

Electronic trading is another term often, and inappropriately associated with HFT. It refers to the ability to transmit orders electronically as opposed to by telephone, mail or in person. Moreover, with the vast majority of orders in the financial markets being conducted by computer this term is currently obsolete.

Algorithmic trading is more complex and refers to a range of algorithms spanning from order-execution process to high-frequency portfolio allocation decision. An execution algorithm would decide how best to route an order to the exchange, the best time to execute a submitted order, and the best sequence of sizes in which the order should be optimally processed. Algorithms generating HFT signals would make portfolio allocation decisions and decision to enter or close a position in a particular security.

As you can see HFT is comprised of a long queue of considerations. The definitions vary even further according to market participants, therefore in order to properly define it for our purposes we will cite relevant

industry definitions and comment on their similarities or
differences line-by-line.

The Technology Subcommittee of the U.S. Commodity Futures
Trading Commission (CFTC) characterized HFT as a form of
automated trading that employs:

- Algorithms for decision making, order initiation,
  generation, routing, or execution, for each
  individual transaction without human direction.
    - The systems are designed to be fully automated
      but do not include considerations for order
      routing.

- Low-latency technology that is designed to minimize
  response times, including proximity and co-location
  services.
    - No such technology or proximity/co-location
      services are required. The systems focus on
      micro-trends and do not require any additional
      technology.

- High-speed connections to markets for order entry.
    - Standard internet connection that allows
      efficient trades on a minimum of 15-second bar
      resolution will suffice.

- High message rates (orders, quotes or
  cancellations).
    - No such consideration is necessary.

Furthermore, a survey of hedge-fund managers conducted by
FINalternative in 2009 focused on the holding period of
capital throughput.

    High-frequency trading compromises

    - Systematic
        - Yes, our approach is systematic.
    - Quant-based models

- Yes, our systems are based on a simple mathematical model.
- With holding periods from a fraction of a second to one day (no position held overnight)
  - Yes, however our systems will run on 15-second and 5-minute bars and no positions will be held overnight.

HFT strategies fall into four general categories:

1. Arbitrage
2. Directional event-based trading
3. Automated market making
4. Liquidity detection

- Our systems fall into the category of Directional Event-Based Trading and more specifically they are directional strategies that identify short-term trends and momentum. However, a case can be made that it is also event-based with consideration to the Covid Era. It would require an acceptance on overlapping the constraints of Macroeconomic and HFT trading principles which I am comfortable with but would require a more esoteric conversation requiring a model available in Econophysics and is beyond the scope of this work.

In closing, please know that the definitions set forth in this chapter are not meant to be definitive in their definition of HFT. They have been curated solely for the purpose of framing the theory and execution of our systems.

What's The Why?

Whenever I am in conversation with someone about trading, business, or the business of trading I like to gauge the energy I will afford the discussion by analyzing the response to one question: What's the why? Three simple words that if properly timed will allow you to peer directly into someone's skillset, abstraction of thought, ability to transfer concepts from plausible to demonstrative, awareness of the calculus of events surrounding us all, and intent. I will leave the skillset calculation to the reader, however, let me explain myself on the remainder.

Abstract of Thought in
Stream of Consciousness

The Covid Era has ushered in, or exposed, the discrepancies of society but for our purpose the financial markets; the novel Coronavirus spread faster and further than we expected, or hoped, before anything resembling a plan came to be; political discord and partisan fighting sent mixed messages, one Democratic, one Republican, and one health professionals; unfortunately we tended to acquiesce to the opinion that suited our personal idealized narrative; it hit New York first and hard, then urban areas; this allowed a large portion of the population to treat Covid-19 as a "Them" problem; the infection rate explodes and the economy shuts down; WTI goes negative for the first time ever; we go from the longest Bull market in history to a Bear market virtually overnight; the FED drops interest rates to 0.00 to 0.25 and then begins to buy up municipal and corporate bonds through ETF producers, a first; stimulus checks go out, extra unemployment is given; people are stuck at home, technology and no-transaction costs turns everyone into a day trader; unemployment hits levels greater than the worst portion of The Great Recession; the markets hit a bottom and soar back after a gradual re-opening; the infection rate skyrockets and becomes 10-fold worse than it was; some States roll back their re-opening; the Nasdaq breaks its all-time record while unemployment remains over 10 percent in the U.S., a service-based economy; there is a problem brewing.

Plausible to Demonstrate

Plausible

There is no precedent for our current era. Any traditional low-frequency quantitative model would assume a series of idealized market conditions. We have no concept of ideal and thus will revert to high-frequency. Moreover, our assessment of relevant public information is that it is all irrelevant because we have no valid gauge. We will need to narrow the window in which we consume information and then build systems that access this data in a binary form in order to construct our own systems of assigning relevance.

Demonstrative

I have created a variable that requires only one bar to calculate. I then compare it to the close of that very same bar in order to place a trade at the open of the very next bar. Moreover, to off-set the necessity for profit-targets and stop-losses every position will only be open for one bar. That is to say that if we buy at the Open of the current bar we will sell at the next bar from the entry.

Our choice of markets will be futures. Being that a futures contract is a liability as opposed to a share in the equities market being an asset it will fundamentally be simpler to gain value from a contract price going up or down. While this is possible with the equities market it requires a level of complexity in the borrowing of shares that does not lend to an ease of execution.

The specific security we will trade will be the E-mini S&P 500 Futures. It trades at $50.00 per full point with a tick-value of 0.25 and a typical transaction cost, depending on your broker, from between $2 to $3. This means that one-tick, the minimal increment equaling $12.50 (0.25 * $50.00), we still have the potential for profitability. Moreover, it is the most liquid futures market on U.S. exchanges and gives up the best potential to enter and exit a long or short trade with minimal regard to slippage. Also, studies have shown that 25 percent of trading in the mini-500 is comprised of high-frequency trading.

Lastly, due to leverage being built into this market it requires less margin (account size) to trade in a high-frequency manner. Once again, depending on your broker, contracts can range from $500 to $1250 and up depending on volatility plus minimum balances and any platform and data fees. To trade at this level of frequency in the equities market would require qualifying as a pattern day trader and maintaining an account balance of $25,000.

Calculus of Events Surrounding Us

There is an amazing amount of debt being issued in order to keep the economy afloat. It is easier to see this translate to the financial markets, but it is not sustainable. Unless we are going to shift our measure of success to one that does not value growth as a determinate factor of success and simultaneously convert to Modern Monetary Theory from Keynesian principles, someone will be left holding the hot potato.

As I write these words it is August 2020. Now we know that the spreading of Covid-19 will not be slowed by the summer heat as we once hoped. As horrendous as it is now, it will be worse in the winter months. This will inevitably increase the potential for another lockdown in which the economy, which is doing poorly, will do worse. At this point, the woes of the economy will transfer to the financial markets.

Evidence is mounting in that financial institutions have begun to keep more cash on hand in order to ease the burden of loan and mortgage defaults they foresee. The moratorium on evictions will not last indefinitely and the strain on the health care system is going to be realized once the State and Federal fiscal years do not produce the sufficient amount of tax-revenue to sustain operations.

We will require a system that is designed to keep its ear as close to the ground as possible.

Intent

Simple. Maintain portfolio viability through any market condition. In unprecedented times we will focus on unique constructions.

The Chauhan Actual Price (CAP)

The Chauhan Actual Price (CAP) is a low-lag, low-pass non-recursive filter with minimal transfer response.

$CAP = High_t * 0.1 + Low_t * 0.1 + Close_t * 0.8$

According to the Nyquist frequency the shortest analysis period that is possible (without aliasing) is a two-bar cycle. Aliasing refers to the false signals that results from under-sampling and is the dominant term used to describe noise in the data of shorter cycle periods. If you think of financial market data in terms of a line being drawn on an x and y-axis in the first quadrant from left to right this would be incorrect. If we use the closing price of a time-bar as representative of that bar then each sample would actually be a dot placed in the quadrant with a line drawn to connect them. Much like a complex game of connect-the-dots.

The CAP challenges the assertion of Nyquist slightly because it does not use a single point of data representative of a time frame over more than one bar. Instead it weighs three of the four price components of a time-bar to construct a single data point. It takes 10 percent of the High plus 10 percent of the Low plus 80 percent of the Close, omitting the Open.

There is a similar variable under various names that reports calculations over a single bar. It is referred to as the Typical Price or Pivot Point.

$TP/PP = H_t * 0.3 + L_t * 0.3 + C_t * 0.3$

Its drawback is that it affords the exact same weight to all three of the information components considered in the price bar. The calculation of this variable displays that the High, Low and Close of a bar are of equal importance.

I disagree. Although the high and low are of relevance they are minimal compared to the close.

The vast majority of indicators such as Stochastics, Relative Strength Index (RSI), Moving Average Convergence/Divergence (MACD), and Bollinger Bands use only the closing price. Some indicators consider volume but none that are viable give equal consideration to the high, low, and close. Therefore, neither will we.

// Covid Era High Frequency Trading
// Systems Explained

{This chapter will be written in the format of an EasyLanguage Development Environment with heavy commentary to explain the various parts.}

[IntrabarOrderGeneration = False]

{The EasyLanguage attribute IntrabarOrderGeneration allows you to turn on or off the intrabar order generation flag. If the attribute is present and set to TRUE, the 'Enable intrabar order generation and calculation' flag will be checked, the checkbox will be disabled, and the radio buttons will be available. If the attribute is present and set to FALSE, the 'Enable intrabar order generation and calculation' flag will be unchecked, and the checkbox and radio button will be disabled.

This attribute is hardcoded here to ensure that it presents in this strategy without having to rely heavily on the setting menu. Also, it allows the reader to convert the functional purpose of this system into another computer language preferred by the user.

We use it here in order to ensure that the variable calculation occurs only once per bar. This point is crucial to reinforce the performance of the system. Unless otherwise specified TradeStation will assess the various computations expressed in the code on a tick-by-tick basis. This would not allow us to use the Open of the bar after the order fill bar to exit the trade.

For testing purposes, we always compute the profit/loss figures that go into the win/loss totals separately for each bar. It is vital that a string of bars having the same position (long or short) not be pooled into a single trade result. The bars must be tallied individually.

The resulting profit factor then produces a reliable, repeatable measure of the variables signal performance that is derived entirely from being computed at as fine a quantization level as possible. For this book we have combined both long and short variable signals into a single trading strategy in order to allow it to be fully implemented.

Lastly, by forcing the strategy to only make one variable calculation and order exit/entry per bar it ensures that a trade will be opened on one bar at the Open and exited on the Open of the next bar. These implementations are of paramount importance when effectively executing these strategies.}

// Variables //

Variables: CAP (0), TimeConsideration (0);

```
  CAP = (High * 0.1) +(Low * 0.1) + (Close * 0.8);
  Value0 = CalcTime (0830, -BarInterval);
  Value1 = CalcTime (1400, -BarInterval);
  IF = (Time >= Value0 AND Time <= 1000) OR
       (Time >= Value1 AND Time <= 1500) THEN
      TimeConsideration = 1 ELSE TimeConsideration = 0;
```

{In futures, open interest is the measurement of those participants with outstanding positions; it is the netting out of all open positions (long and short sales) in any one market or delivery month and gives an understanding of the depth of participation and anticipated value. Unlike the stock market, which can only trade a fixed number of outstanding shares, the futures market can add net contracts for every new buyer and short seller and reduce the interest in the market when both buyers and sellers liquidate.

Futures volume can create very different results from volume for stocks. Futures volume comes in two parts, contract volume and total volume. Contract volume begins at zero, increases as the contract moves from deferred

(many months away from delivery) to nearby delivery, then
back to zero as the contract expires. In the same way,
futures data shows contract open interest and total open
interest. That data varies in the same pattern as volume;
however, open interest is much more stable than volume.
Similar to volume, open interest increases as market
activity increases and reflects a similar fundamental
value.

For the purpose of an HFT system we will not consider using
volume or open-interest because of a lack of signal
information that reports on a high-resolution basis. Tick-
volume is what we will use to specify the times of day
that we will allow our trading system to calculate trading
signals. Tick volume is the number of recorded price
changes, regardless of volume or size of the price change
that occurs during any time interval. Tick volume relates
directly to actual volume because, as the market becomes
more active, prices move back and forth from bid to ask
more often. It then becomes apparent that frequency of
price changes is directly related to the actual volume
traded.

We chose the time frame in which to allow the system to
trade for one main reason, tick-volume pattern. With
concern to tick-volume pattern the Mini-500 tends to have
a very symmetric U-shaped pattern. Most price changes per
time-frame occur at the open and close of the broad market
(0930 to 1600 EST) with the bottom falling during midday.
At 1000 CST the tick volume is roughly equivalent to the
close at 1500 CST using 15-minute bars, thus qualifying
the end of our first session. The second session from 1400
to 1500 CST was chosen by counting backward from the close
by one-hour while the first trading trading session counts
forward to 1000 CST.}

                        // Long Entry //

IF TimeConsideration THEN BEGIN
        IF CAP < Close THEN
                BUY ("Long#1") next bar Open;

```
                                                        END;
```

{The variable signal is that the CAP value is less-than the Close price of the specified time bar. This indicates the potential for the price to increase from the current bar to one bar in the future.

// Long Exit //

```
IF MarketPosition = 1 THEN SELL this bar Close;
```

{Here we use the MarketPosition reserved word in order to tie the Exit to the Entry. This allows us to exit our trade at the first available price of the next bar with this bar close specifying the bar that forms directly after the entry bar.

// Short Entry //

```
IF TimeConsideration THEN BEGIN
      IF CAP > Close THEN
            SellShort ("Short#1") next bar Open;
                                                        END;
```

{The variable signal is that the CAP value is greater-than the Close price of the specified time bar. This indicated the potential for the price to decrease from the current bar to one bar in the future}

// Short Exit //

```
IF MarketPosition = -1 BuyToCover this bar Close;
```

EasyLanguage Source Code

```
// Covid Era HFT CAP >< Close Trading System#1
// Author: Vikram Singh Chauhan
// Security: E-Mini S&P 500 Futures
// Timebar: 15-Seconds

{As you'll notice the strategy code has been chopped down
a bit in order to eliminate redundancies and increase
operating efficiency.}

[ IntrabarOrderGeneration = False ]

Value0 = H * 0.1 + L * 0.1 + C * 0.8;
IF (Time >= 0829 AND Time <= 1000) OR
   (Time >= 1359 AND Time <= 1500) THEN
    Condition0 = 1 ELSE Condition0 = 0;

IF Condition0 THEN BEGIN
     IF Value0 < C THEN
          BUY ("Long#1") next bar Open;
                                        END;

IF MarketPosition = 1 SELL this bar C;

IF Condition0 THEN BEGIN
     IF Value0 > C THEN
          SellShort ("Short#1") next bar Open;
                                        End;

IF MarketPosition = -1 BuyToCover this bar Close;
```

System #1 Performance Summary

	All Trades	Long Trades	Short Trades
Total Net Profit	$81,987.50	$46,000.00	$35,987.50
Gross Profit	$2,064,000.00	$1,034,287.50	$1,029,712.50
Gross Loss	($1,982,012.50)	($988,287.50)	($993,725.00)
Profit Factor	1.04	1.05	1.04
Roll Over Credit	$0.00	$0.00	$0.00
Open Position P/L	$0.00	$0.00	$0.00
Select Total Net Profit	$78,187.50	$22,562.50	$55,625.00
Select Gross Profit	$1,810,787.50	$885,975.00	$924,812.50
Select Gross Loss	($1,732,600.00)	($863,412.50)	($869,187.50)
Select Profit Factor	1.05	1.03	1.06
Adjusted Total Net Profit	$61,731.65	$31,658.85	$21,682.49
Adjusted Gross Profit	$2,053,659.17	$1,026,956.18	$1,022,419.66
Adjusted Gross Loss	($1,991,927.52)	($995,297.34)	($1,000,737.16)
Adjusted Profit Factor	1.03	1.03	1.02
Total Number of Trades	94,038	47,025	47,013
Percent Profitable	42.36%	42.32%	42.41%
Winning Trades	39,839	19,903	19,936
Losing Trades	39,960	19,877	20,083
Even Trades	14,239	7,245	6,994

System #1 Performance Graph - Equity Line Curve

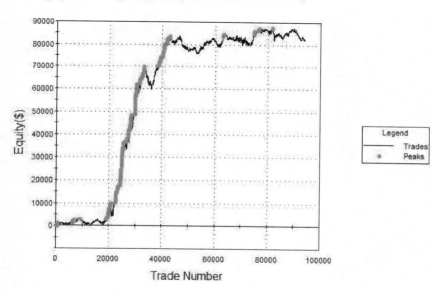

Equity Curve Line - @ESU20 15 sec.(1/9/2020 17:00:15 - 8/7/2020 16:00)

System #1 Performance Graph – Equity Curve Underwater (weekly)

Equity Curve Underwater(weekly) - @ESU20 15 sec.(1/9/2020 17:00:15 - 8/7/2020 16:00)

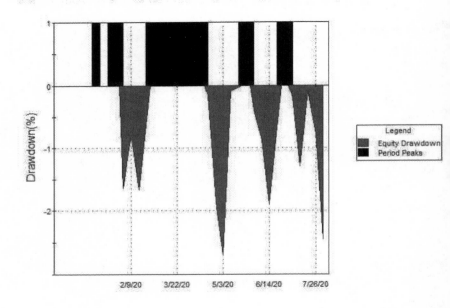

System #1 Performance Graph — Monthly Net Profit

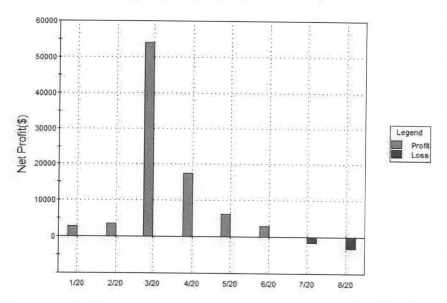

```
// Covid Era HFT CAP >< Close Trading System#2
// Author: Vikram Singh Chauhan
// Security: E-Mini S&P 500 Futures
// Timebar: 5-Minutes

{At the 5-minute frequency the CAP >< Close relationship
changes so that Value0 (CAP) > Close is a long signal and
Value0 (CAP) < Close is a short signal. This is the exact
opposite of the 15-second system.}

          [ IntrabarOrderGeneration = False ]

Value0 = H * 0.1 + L * 0.1 + C * 0.8;
IF (Time >= 0825 AND Time <= 1000) OR
   (Time >= 1355 AND Time <= 1500) THEN
    Condition0 = 1 ELSE Condition = 0;

IF Condition0 THEN BEGIN
     IF Value0 > C THEN
          BUY ("Long#2") next bar Open;
                                        END;
IF MarketPosition = 1 SELL this bar Close;

If Condition0 THEN BEGIN
     IF Value0 < C THEN
          SellShort ("Short#2") next bar Open;
                                        END;
IF MarketPosition = -1 BuyToCover this bar Close;
```

System #2 Performance Summary

	All Trades	Long Trades	Short Trades
Total Net Profit	$41,587.50	$22,875.00	$18,712.50
Gross Profit	$500,450.00	$268,337.50	$232,112.50
Gross Loss	($458,862.50)	($245,462.50)	($213,400.00)
Profit Factor	1.09	1.09	1.09
Roll Over Credit	$0.00	$0.00	$0.00
Open Position P/L	($100.00)	$0.00	($100.00)
Select Total Net Profit	$20,812.50	$6,712.50	$14,100.00
Select Gross Profit	$411,150.00	$246,737.50	$164,412.50
Select Gross Loss	($390,337.50)	($240,025.00)	($150,312.50)
Select Profit Factor	1.05	1.03	1.09
Adjusted Total Net Profit	$18,916.87	$7,925.29	$562.64
Adjusted Gross Profit	$489,134.43	$260,676.97	$223,515.74
Adjusted Gross Loss	($470,217.56)	($252,751.68)	($222,953.10)
Adjusted Profit Factor	1.04	1.03	1.00
Total Number of Trades	3,678	2,426	1,252
Percent Profitable	53.18%	50.58%	58.23%
Winning Trades	1,956	1,227	729
Losing Trades	1,633	1,134	499
Even Trades	89	65	24

System #2 Performance Graph - Equity Curve Line

Equity Curve Line - @ESU20 5 min.(1/1/2020 17:05 - 8/7/2020 16:00)

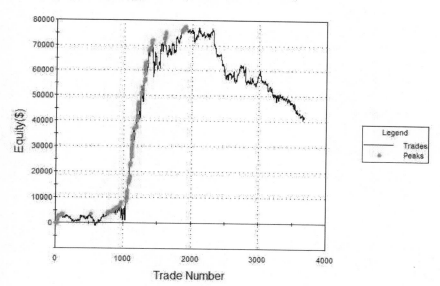

System #2 Performance Graph – Equity Curve Underwater (weekly)

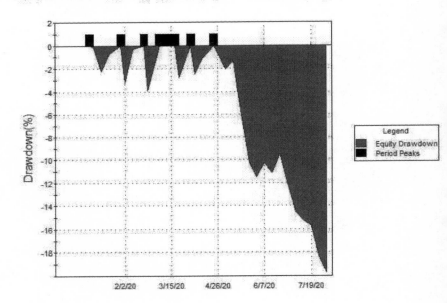

System #2 Performance Graph - Monthly Net Profit

Monthly Net Profit - @ESU20 5 min.(1/1/2020 17:05 - 8/7/2020 16:00)

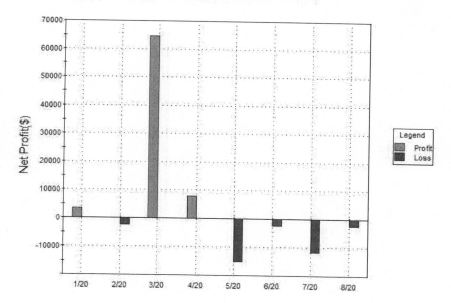

Conclusion

As it stands, I have never typed a single piece of code into any computer. My only tool has been my faithful Casio fx-260 Solar Calculator. The challenges have been formidable, but I am so grateful to have been afforded unconventional access to this industry. It has forced me to learn how to compute every publicly available technical market indicator available by hand. This has been a blessing in disguise because it has made me intimately familiar with even the tiniest nuances.

I have placed this explanation in the back of the book because it is my prayer that you would assess the work before criticizing the source. Being in prison and a man of color can offer society the ability to place me in a void while being able to remain untouched by self-conscious scorn. Rightfully so, with regard to the former, in some cases.

This work and this admission stand to serve as the expression of my incontestable contrition for the crimes I have committed. I apologize to society and my victims. I did not, nor would I have ever, caused physical harm to anyone but being a Combat Veteran of two wars diagnosed with Post Traumatic Stress Disorder and Traumatic Brain Injury along with multiple other combat injuries, I understand that some of the deepest scars we suffer do not leave marks.
I am resolved to spend the remainder of my life to the benefit of society. Thank you for your support.

If you would like to contact me directly please send your correspondence to the address listed below. Otherwise you can write to the e-mail or Twitter account listed at the front of this book, my mother checks it every day.

> Note: No color paper or stickers (including address labels) are allowed. Only white or lined paper, handwritten or typed. I apologize for the inconvenience.

Vikram Singh Chauhan
TDJC NO:02096044
Wallace Unit
1675 South FM 3525
Colorado City, TX 79512

References

Aldridge, Irene, 2013. "High-Frequency Trading: A Practical Guide to Algorithmic Strategies and Trading Systems". Second Edition. Wiley.

Florescu, I., Mariani, M., Stanley, H., Viens, F., 2016. "Handbook of High Frequency Trading And Modeling In Finance." Wiley.

Garner, Carley, 2017. "A Trader's First Book On Commodities: Everything You Need To Know About Futures and Options Trading Before Placing A Trade." Decarley Trading.

Harris, Sunny J., 2011. "TradeStation Made Easy!: Using EasyLanguage To Build Profits With The Most Popular Trading Software." Wiley Trading.

Kaufman, Perry J., 2013. "Trading Systems And Methods + Website." Fifth Edition. Wiley.

Masters, Timothy, 2020. "Statistically Sound Indicators for Financial Market Prediction: Algorithms in C++." Masters.

Made in the USA
Columbia, SC
25 October 2020